City
Streets
to
Destiny

City Streets to Destiny

Autobiography
By
P. Durrell Nathan

E-BookTime, LLC
Montgomery, Alabama

City Streets to Destiny

ISBN: 1-59824-282-2

First Edition
Published July 2006
E-BookTime, LLC
6598 Pumpkin Road
Montgomery, AL 36108
www.e-booktime.com

Dedicated To

Michelle, my wife, who looked beyond my faults, disregarded my past, and embraced my future. Thank you for believing in me, and my talents. You have been a friend, partner, and companion. You are the white rose in the garden of my heart. Your beautiful smile and warm laughter echoes in my spirit. Truly, this is forever............

To The Reader

The characters in this book are true but their real names have been changed. The events portrayed occurred exactly as they are revealed. This is a true story. The facts of my testimony are conveyed without compromise in the hope that you, the reader, will in some way relate or be inspired.

–P. Durrell Nathan

Contents

Introduction

The objective of this book is to offer hope for a better life for anyone facing overwhelming odds and challenges. Here, I take you on a journey into the threshold of my life down the corridors of darkness, despair, and destruction into the realm of light, life, and the love of God. From the shadows of death to the towers of victory, from ashes to beauty. My story will inspire you with faith, hope, and optimism. You don't have to stay the way you are, or where you are. You can change, you can transition yourself for a brighter tomorrow. It's not too late for you. All you have to do is begin to see yourself differently. Begin to think differently about yourself. Believe that God loves you and has a better life in store for you. Whether you're in prison, divorced, poor, a struggling single parent, suicidal, bankrupt, depressed, bound by drugs and alcohol addiction, sick or battling a disease, confused, physically or verbally abused as a child, sexually abused, raped, falsely accused or convicted, abandoned by your parents, betrayed by friends, or no matter what you have gone through and may be facing today, I want you to know that you have a destiny to discover and purpose on this earth to fulfill. God has a plan for your life. He wants to give you more than what you have, take you where you've never been, show you what you've never seen, and help you fulfill your dreams. He desires for you to go beyond what you can imagine. How hungry are you for more? How desperate are you for a better life?

Perhaps you are financially secure and have much but feel so empty in your heart. I challenge you to pray and ask God to fill that void in your life. I encourage you to read this book and be inspired to discover your destiny.

Prayer

Petitions
Released
At
Your
Earnest
Request

Chapter 1

Childhood

In the year of 1985 crack-cocaine hit the city of Mount Vernon like the Atomic bomb had hit Hiroshima, Japan. The lives of countless thousands were about to change dramatically for the worse, and potentially forever. A man weighing 300-pounds could lose close to 100 pounds in just a little over a week, while not eating properly, and nearly selling everything he owned, just to buy more crack! The drug itself would absorb the appetite, causing extreme physical imbalance, as well as dependency and chronic addiction.

One Saturday morning I awoke to do my typical Saturday morning agenda; prepare my cereal, watch cartoons, then go outside to play with friends. I got out of bed to brush my teeth, and to wash my face. From the bathroom I made my way to the kitchen where I climbed up on to the counter to obtain the cereal from the cupboard. While viewing the contents of the cabinet, I noticed something distinctly wrapped in aluminum foil with what appeared to be a glass stem protruding from it. I opened it and discovered what appeared to be a pipe. As I studied it, I noticed residue. A white powdery substance. What I saw took my breath away. It was a crack pipe! I was horrified to find out that my Mom had been using crack-cocaine.

Tragically, this was the cold, harsh reality of many children my age at that time in my young life. This book was written to inspire the millions of people who can in some way identify with my story. This account is told like it is without the intention of offending anyone. The reality of these documented events are shared and experienced by untold millions of children in America and throughout the world.

In autumn of 1977, shortly after midnight, on Sunday October 23, Phillip Durrell Nathan was born at the Mount Vernon hospital, located in the city of Mt. Vernon, N. Y. I weighed in at 8 pounds. My mom was 23 when she gave birth to me. By this time, my older brother Kevin was already 4 years of age. We didn't have the same dad. Tragically, Kevin's dad had committed suicide before my brother had been born. This had a devastating effect on his life and future. My mom later met Kevin Mcgaha, the man who would later become my dad, as well as my sister's. My Mom and dad had called it quits when I was about five. They reunited for a brief period during which time my precious sister Dwann was conceived. Shortly thereafter, they decided to go there own separate ways, resulting in a bitter split between the two. From then on I wouldn't see my dad for years. To me, he was a man in the shadows of life. He made no effort to show up at any point in my life when I needed him. He lived his life and went to his grave without ever reconciling with my sister and me.

As kids, we had it rough in every sense of the word. Times were very tough. We grew up in harsh circumstances. My mother was a single parent, uneducated, on welfare, and addicted to crack-cocaine. We lived in sheer poverty. At some point in her life she descended in to a deep depression from which she wouldn't recover for many years. It became her handicap that prevented her from nurturing us in the love, affection, care, and support that children need. She had become almost totally emotionally detached from us. I became very isolated, developed poor self-esteem, and a shattered self-image. I was very insecure as a young boy. I experienced much hurt. I gradually began to fear my mother due to the physical and verbal abuse. Eventually, I became resentful and bitter toward her. Quite frankly, it got to a point where I really hated my mom. The conditions we were living under, multiplied by the abuse and neglect had a major negative Impact on my life.

In the early days growing up my brother Kevin was always on the go, out trying to make ends meet for himself, my sister, and I. He had become the man of the house. He'd bring home all sorts of "goodies" with him. We'd go to bed eating "now and later" candy to sometimes substitute for the dinner meal we didn't have that evening. When I say we were poor, I mean we were poor! There were days that we went to bed hungry. Whenever we did have a meal, the lack of sufficiency left a lingering sensation of hunger. I was a very skinny kid growing up. I recall my fifth grade teacher Mr. Gorshoffe often telling me that I was the skinniest kid in his class. There was a growing concern. He wondered about me. For my sixth grade graduation I wore clothes that were given to me by two friends. I was subject to much humiliation and scorn by fellow classmates during the graduation ceremony. Word got out that I was wearing someone else's shoes, slacks, and dress shirt. I was ridiculed in such a humiliating manner!

I managed to keep my composure and get through the shameful experience. At home, we seldom had any toys. On many occasions, Kevin, along with friends would go to "H.L. Greens" and "Genovese" to steal action figure toys (G.I. Joe, Star Wars, etc) so we'd have toys at home to play with. I'll never forget the fateful and dreadful day of his apprehension, the day he got busted! The local police came to my home one evening and broke the news to my Mom. They couldn't call us because a telephone was an uncommon convenience around the house. We very rarely had a phone, much less keep the bill paid if we did get one. Living at home was like living in the early 1800's. You may find this funny, but it's the truth. If you wanted to contact the Nathan family you'd have to walk to our home or contact us by mail. Thus, the police had decided to send a patrol car to our residence. My Mom had to take a ride with the police down to the station to get Kevin. She was furious. After arriving back home, the repercussions went beyond appropriate measures of discipline, leading to physical abuse. Later that evening Kevin revealed to me the awful bruises that were swollen on his buttocks, thighs, and calf, all of which were dark red, black, and a dark purple color. From that period onward I began to fear my mother at greater levels. I became literally afraid of her in every sense of the word. When I tell you I was scared, I mean I was terrified! Sadly, this type of physical abuse continued in both our lives, combined with verbal abuse. I recall almost being paralyzed, losing sensation in both my legs for a short period while being beaten by my Mom with a hard-plastic standard sized baseball bat. The abuse later led too much of the rebellion in our lives. We went through hard times. I was glad for my sister's sake that she was still very young, and hadn't experienced the abuse we had. By the time that Kevin had reached the age of twelve, he'd already made up his mind that he was ready to leave home. I could see the pain in his eyes. He hated the way we lived. On one occasion I recalled him stating that he hated our home. I couldn't blame him. My mother had many personal problems of her own, which had a major impact on my brother, sister, and me. At the time, she was battling many of her own demons. People can be so overwhelmed with things in life that they'll begin to abuse that which they cherish, either their own children, siblings, or themselves, ultimately even committing suicide. This is real life folks. This is not a fictitious story out of a novel. This is my story and I want to share it with you in the hope that it will bring inspiration to you, making you aware that you don't stand-alone in the dark shadows of life.

As my brother entered Middle School (7th grade), many of his peers were already engaged in smoking marijuana, and dealing drugs. While only twelve years old, Kevin was already introduced to drug deals at school.

Kevin began selling drugs in order to put food on the table for his kid brother and sister. It wasn't long before he had become aware of our mother's drug use. Sometime, Mom would send him to a girl friend's house named Rhonda accompanied by a note to take to her. My brother indicated to me that he would read these letters/notes, finding that Mom was requesting drugs from her girlfriend. Many children in our neighborhood were facing the same cold, harsh, reality. Our parents were addicted to crack cocaine! They would do absolutely anything to get it. This meant no Christmas gifts, birthday gifts, school shopping for new clothes, no furniture for our home, nor any toys. Our childhood had become a nightmare. All the money went to the drug dealer who stood on the corner. As the years went on, we'd notice that the small amount of furniture that we did possess, along with household appliances, would gradually disappear. We later learned that our Mom had sold these elements in order to support her intense drug habit. If she was working at the time, her paycheck would be consumed to buy more drugs. If she was getting the monthly welfare check from the government, this was also squandered on drugs. Whatever the case was, any income always went to the drug dealer.

Whenever Mom couldn't afford to get high she would take it out on us. My brother was seldom home. He had become a drug dealer himself. He'd be out all night striving to make a living and to provide for my sister and I.. He refused to give my Mom any of the money he'd make. He knew she would only use it to buy more drugs. I know for some of you it is hard to imagine that a mere twelve year old could be a drug dealer. This is the reality for thousands of young African Americans all across the country.

My sister was too young to comprehend the nightmare we were living in. Much of my mother's wrath fell upon me. My brother was rarely home, Dwann was very young and tender, so I found myself being the subject of much verbal and physical abuse. My Mom constantly cursed at me when talking to me. I was beaten very often. I was literally terrified of my Mom. Whenever I got a spanking for something it was always harsh and abusive. Each beating always left me feeling as if I wasn't wanted, as though my Mom regretted having me. You cherish what you love. You don't abuse it. You destroy the value in whatever you abuse. It's one thing to discipline a child with tenuous reprimand and a spanking for the sole intent of correction, but it's another thing to curse at your child and physically abuse them. For you parents out there, I admonish you, please do not curse at your child nor physically abuse them. They will bear the emotional scars and recollection for the rest of their lives. Healing is always possible. However, the pain which precedes the healing process is inevitable. I recall one occasion when my Mom had beaten me with a yellow plastic standard size baseball bat! She nearly paralyzed me. I can vividly remember partially losing sensation in my legs and lower back. I yelled out to her saying that I couldn't feel my legs, then she suddenly stopped beating me. My sense of feeling gradually returned, as my Mom departed my bedroom. From that day forward I hated my Mom. I seriously wanted to kill her. One day I proposed a plot to my cousin Marvin, but he insisted that he'd have nothing to do with her murder. He walked away from me telling me that I was crazy. I wasn't crazy. I was simply terrified and fearful of my Mother. I felt that I'd have to kill her in order to stop the beatings! At some point I began to stop caring about anybody and everything.

The abuse, having no food, the sheer deep poverty and neglect began to have a tremendous impact on my life. At times, my Mom would leave home while my sister and I were left alone by ourselves. I'd wake up some mornings and my Mom would be gone. I recall being afraid and lonely. Life simply didn't add up. What was a child to do?

School life for me was great. I enjoyed attending school. Not because I achieved good grades. How could a child focus academically in school while living in hell at home? School was an outlet for me to get away from what was going on in my household. I met many friends at school, especially considering that many were taken by my sense of humor. I joined the percussion program, participated in the all-city orchestra band, which is one of the very few highlights of my childhood. It was so complicated to concentrate on my grades. Mom rarely did the laundry, so I was obliged to wear the same old dirty clothes and funky socks to school at least three times a week. I was so embarrassed at school. Whenever I'd go over to a friend's house to play Nintendo after school I'd be ashamed to remove my sneakers when entering. The odor emanating from my dirty socks was strong enough to knock someone unconscious! Amid school hours, to keep the other kids from making fun of me, I decided that I'd become a "Joker", to make everyone laugh. And it worked! I gained many friends this way. I was tired of the other kids teasing me, calling me "dirty dee".

I struggled with my homework. I had no one to assist me. Mom didn't have a High School education. I ended up getting a lot of failing grades. At last, I'd decided that I wouldn't take it anymore! I started contemplating how I could make it on my own. I would sneak out of the house late at night looking for a way to get a meal. My brother would go to a different state to sell more drugs to earn more money.

My life was about to take a dangerous and dramatic turn!

One afternoon I was outside playing with a friend, Akeem, along with two other friends in the local day care center play ground. My brother had recently come back in to town. Suddenly, my friends and I heard police sirens. What I saw next shocked me! I noticed a subject climbing over the fence in an attempt to elude a pursuing police officer chasing him. To my utter amazement, the individual was actually my brother! As he ran, he was spitting crack-cocaine vials from his mouth, some of which he had managed to swallow. I was gripped with apprehension, I was so afraid for him. I couldn't believe my eyes. I couldn't believe what was happening. All of a sudden, Akeem and my other friends began to cheer for my brother saying, "go Kevin, go, he's gaining on you, run faster". I beheld the scene as it appeared to be a movie in reality playing out before my very eyes. Kevin exited the day care center playground with the police officer in hot pursuit. My friends and I decided to follow the chase, which ended a few blocks away. As we approached the scene, Kevin lay flat on the ground in handcuffs. We made brief eye contact, from the looks of his eyes I knew he was apologizing to me and wanted me to notify our mother. Akeem, my friends, and I fled the scene, running as fast as we could to my house. After arriving home and telling my Mom, her response was, "so, I don't care, that's his problem". Those words sunk deep within my heart. I was so hurt. My Mom was so indifferent about the situation. I was blown away by her apathy, and lack of concern for my brother. Afterward, I went out of the house to meet with my friends. Akeem had asked what did my Mom have to say. I quickly made up a lie because I was too ashamed, humiliated to tell him what my Mom had really said. I knew Akeem could relate. He was my closest friend at the time. His Mom was also addicted to crack-cocaine. This was common among many of my childhood friends. My brother Kevin spent the next eighteen months in a Juvenile Detention Center. Deep down inside I knew he'd be okay. Kevin was always capable of holding his own.

Amid Kevin's incarceration, I'd spent long summers missing him, as we grew further apart. Finally, eighteen months had expired. Nothing had changed about Mom and our family conditions. My brother was released and it was great having him home again. Sadly, our reunion was rather short lived. Kevin's feelings had not changed. He still resented living at home, the poverty, circum-stances, conditions, under which we were still living. He soon packed his things and moved to Raleigh North Carolina where he'd become a career drug dealer, earning tens of thousands of dollars. By this time I was eleven years, my sister was just five, my brother was only fifteen.

Though we were all just kids, still very young, the tragedy is that we were exposed to many terrible things at a tender age. I tell my story in the hope that some young girl or boy in America or around the globe may get a hold of this book and discover inspiration and encouragement in knowing that there is a living God who can break the chains of poverty, abuse, discouragement, despair, depression, suicide, and hopelessness. If God could reach me, he can reach you, or your child, siblings and family. God is love. And He loves you. It is no coincidence that you are reading this book. My life is real. What I endured in my horrible childhood was real. But, there is a God that is more real than any thing we could ever encounter. Open your heart to him. He's only a prayer away.

I soon began middle school. It wasn't long before my started sending money via western union. However, my sister and I weren't seeing any of it. Although it was drug money, I didn't care. I was only concerned about survival. Mom always made vain promises to Dwann and I, saying she'd take us shopping, or that she'd put it to good use, which was never the case. All the money, every dime and cent was actually squandered on crack! My sister and I continued to wear rags, dirty clothes, going day after day without our necessities. We were very neglected. My mother's drug addiction continued to worsen. When my brother did finally come to see us again my sister and I were thrilled. It was like seeing a celebrity. After finding out that Mom was still using drugs he stopped sending the money. He'd thought that it was just some sort of phase she'd been going through but he was badly mistaken. Mom was still using drugs. After staying with us for about a week or so, he departed back to his newfound life in Raleigh North Carolina. I couldn't blame him. He needed to get away. I began to feel that it was time for me to do the same.

At Franco Middle School I met scores of new friends. By this time I still had been associated with an old friend from sixth grade named Eric. I was twelve. Eric was about four years older than I was. He was a young professional car thief. I'd managed to make it through middle school but both my seventh and eighth grade years were spent partially on stealing cars, working for a "chop shop" in the Bronx, N.Y. I started out as a "look out boy" and gradually made my way up. I made my superiors respect me. They saw the sheer hunger in the eyes of a young kid who only wanted to survive and have a better life, something far beyond the reach o poverty. Eric promised to have my back, to take care of me, he knew what my situation was like and was sort of going through much of the same himself. Things were awful at home for him too. My job was to watch out for the police and to also assist in the process of the theft in anyway that I could In order to make fifty bucks in my pocket for the night. While I didn't make much money, I became intrigued by the mere notion of stealing a car so that I could obtain the knowledge for myself, then venture out on my own. Eric and I stole numerous vehicles from various cities. We'd take up to 3 or 4 cars a night, on a good night. The vehicles ranged from BMW, Toyota, Mazda, Jeeps, Nissan, etc, you name it. Whatever the "chop shop" ordered, we went out to steal it. I started to make more money and felt a sense of power because I was taking care of myself and wasn't even yet a teenager. At that tender age, my "m-o" was that I gotta do what I gotta do. I didn't care what people thought of me. I was a reject, neglected by both my parents, and family. My self-esteem was out the window. I cared about one thing, survival. From that point in my childhood I'd decided to go "full time" in to the street life. By any means necessary I had to eat.

One day I received the news that the "chop shop" had been raided and shut down. Eric was among all the other associates that were given long prison sentences and were sent off to jail. The police began cracking down on grand auto theft so I decided to give it a rest for a while. Eric spent the next two years in a juvenile detention center. Meanwhile, I resolved to start pursuing the girls, while connecting with a few other friends. Randy was a popular kid with a sense of humor. Everyone liked him. He had an apartment all to himself in the basement of his grandmother's house. He introduced me to marijuana and drinking. I began drinking and getting high somewhere around age thirteen. We'd get drunk, go out to meet some fine young girls at a house party somewhere, smoke some weed, then bring them back to his basement apartment to have sex with them. We even had orgies! The devil had a hold on our lives at a very young age because of what we were exposed to. Our parents failed to shield, guide, gird, and guard us from the dangers within our society and community. As a result, any child will no doubt go wayward. The reason Randy was living with his grandmother was because his Mom was also a crack head and gave him up. Thus, his precious grandmother had taken custody of him and his older brother Harold. Randy and I knew we'd had it going on. We were hot! We would dress alike sometime, considered ourselves brothers, and vowed to fight for one another. I thought Randy was a bit crazy. He even owned a gun. It was a small 6-shot 22 caliber pistol revolver. We decided that we'd keep it hidden until we needed it for our protection. Unfortunately, our bond was rather short lived. Randy decided to move out to Yonkers with one of his girlfriends. He indicated that he also had a connection out there that would bring in some big cash dealing drugs. I told him that he has my blessing and that he's gotta do what he's gotta do. We vowed to keep in touch, and went our separate ways. I'd always had a love for sports, particularly, football. So I decided to sign up and join the Mount Vernon Razorbacks Football team. I figured it would keep me out of trouble for a while. Or so I hoped.

Chapter 2

Football Season

In August of 1990 I began tryouts for the Mount Vernon Razorbacks. During training camp I managed to do well enough to make the team. I was given the position of cornerback. Coach Wayne had seen in me the ability to cover and defend wide receivers. My teammates were all rejects from within the surrounding community. We all had come from broken homes, plagued with problems, poverty, and drug addict parents. It was a tremendous task for the team coaching staff. It was tough to take in a bunch of dysfunctional kids off the streets and to incorporate us into one solid unit. Many of us couldn't pay for the football equipment so some of the coaching staff pitched in order to pay any or all fees. Each day, football practice proved to be very challenging for my teammates and I. Every single day we gave the coaches a very hard time. We'd fight, argue, arrive to practice late, and when we did show up on time we were high from smoking pot! I believe the staff sympathized with the troubled kids who were on the team, which is why they never chose to cut any of us from the team or send us home. Despite the odds highly stacked against us, they were willing to give us a shot. And for that I am eternally grateful. At the start of the regular season, we lost our first game. Then, we went on to lose all the rest, except one. Our record was 1-9. We only won one single game throughout the entire season. We stunk! I decided that I would return the following season to redeem myself. My teammates and I made a pact that we'd all return the following season to try out for the same team to get revenge on all the teams that had beaten us the previous year. We were determined to have a winning season. The 1991 season had finally come. It was time to enter training camp. I recognized many familiar faces on registration day. I was very independent as a boy. I had to be because Mom was never there. It turned out the coach Tate happened to be an old friend who had grown up with my uncle Sunnie. He recognized my last name and ended up assisting me with the paper work for registration and even sponsored me! I was so elated. Most of the coaching staff from the previous year had returned except coach Mark. He was a ladies man type of coach. He had a lot of woman. I always knew he wouldn't stick around. I never understood what his intent was out on that football field. He'd talk to us more about women than football. I decided that I'd assume the same position I had the previous year which was cornerback. I also was granted the privilege of playing wide receiver on offense. I was now playing both offense and defense. We concluded our season with a 7-3 record. Seven wins, only three losses. We were thrilled! The team and the entire coaching staff went crazy! We had redeemed ourselves from the prior losing season we'd had. My teammates and I had become winners for the first time in our lives. We were a family. I felt at home among those guys. Our coaches believed in us. We prayed together before games, bled together, got injured together, laughed together, won and lost together, and even cried together. I will never forget the experience for as long as I live! It was then on that football field that I actually felt human, loved, or cared about. For me it was one of the few highlights of my childhood. The coaching staff and my teammates had a major impact on my life.

Chapter 3

Crime and Violence

After football season had ended, I was hurled back into the street life. By then, I had just turned 15. Mom was still battling her drug addiction, rarely home, so as always I was left to fend for myself. My sister Dwann was nine years old, still spending much of her time in Yonkers, N.Y. at my aunt's home. My aunt Connie had nine children to look after. Eight boys, one girl, with whom my sister would play with. Connie was hard working single Mom who'd managed to raise her many kids. She never used a drug in her life, at least not to my knowledge. Her last dime was spent on those kids. She loved and took care of them as best as she could. To this day I have enormous respect for her. Meanwhile, my brother Kevin was still in North Carolina. We continued to grow further apart from one another. There were times when I'd think about God, whether He existed or not. Each time I'd dismiss the thought, for I began to believe that He wasn't real. I'd say to myself, "If there were a God, then why is my life the way it is, why is there such turmoil in the world?" Soon after, I begin to feel that if there was a God, I wanted absolutely nothing to do with Him. In essence, I turned my anger and resentment toward Him. From that point on, I blamed God for everything! I'd decided that there'd be no turning back, I'd be fully engaged in "street activity" in order to secure my welfare and survival!

It was December 1992, Christmas and the New Year were approaching. I need some cash for the holidays, basically to take care of myself, for I had no one to look to but myself. My cousin Donald had recently been released from prison. He and I could perfectly relate to each other. His mom Carol and mine used drugs together, and they were very close. Donald was her only child.

When he and I crossed paths he indicated to me that he'd had drug-dealing connections on the streets that would ensure us a large sum of money which would put us in a position to take care of ourselves. You see, I am in no way glorifying the life style of a drug dealer. I had simply become the product of my environment. God knows, I did not choose the circumstances under which I was born, and neither did anyone else who can identify with my testimony. I am being as straight forward as possible to tell my story in the hope that someone will get a hold of this book and find not only inspiration, but the Lord Jesus Christ, who is able to turn around any life or situation! When my cousin presented me with the drug deal, I accepted. It was the only way I knew how to earn money for myself to provide for my necessities. Every other kid on the block who had no mom or dad there to guide them, nor any mentor, they all fell victim to the "game" or the "hustle" (dealing drugs). My cousin and I arranged a day to meet on a mutual occasion. When I arrived at his house he gave me a drug package of crack cocaine to distribute on the streets. We agreed on his percentage of the deal, the amount of money that I'd have to render unto him. He also divulged to me a 12-guage sawed off shotgun, along with a pistol. I was informed that if I ever had any trouble on the streets to simply come to his house for any one of the guns. From that day forward I had decided to not only sell drugs, but I'd also be a "stick-up kid" (one who robs other drug dealers, but also anyone else if need be). This is the mentality of those on the streets. I had become one of them at a very young age for my survival in order to have a meal each day, clothes on my and a roof over my head. Although I'd made money dealing drugs, I had become more fascinated with doing robberies at gunpoint. I enjoyed doing this because as a drug dealer you had to stand on the corner all day long to wait for a sell while risking your freedom. The police can emerge from anywhere, chase you down and throw you in jail. On the contrary, as a stick-up kid, one could just rob another drug dealer and take all his money. The drug dealer wasn't going to report you to the police, nor did you have to stand on the corner taking any risk. Thus, eventually, I stopped selling drugs all together so that I could just embark fully on my newfound occupation at the time. Stick-up missions had become a job for me and a few of my associates, while a few others chose to resume dealing drugs. Victor, Tony, Big Mike, Willie, and Trevor were all new friends. I had known Chris, Shawn, Damion, and Tommy for years. We all grew up together. The ten of us formed a solid unit of loyalty, drug dealing, grand auto theft, robberies, among other crimes to name a few. This was my new found family. The number one law was that if you snitched, you died. Snitches got stitches. We lived by this motto. If you got caught for anything by the authorities, you were to keep your mouth shut and take the weight!

We robbed people at gunpoint on average almost every other day. I was the ringleader. I planned or was behind every mission or operation. We owned several assault weapons, handguns, and semi-automatic weapons, including bulletproof vests. We had connections from New York, down the east coast throughout the south. We were getting larger, and were feared due to the violent reputation that preceded us. We were known as the "Fulton Ave Family." We wreaked havoc within the city limits of Mount Vernon, N.Y. We sold cars through "chop shops", engaged in gun trafficking, partied almost every night, smoked pot, drank beer, liquor, snorted cocaine, and made time for the ladies whenever we could. Although I was very young, I hung out with some people who were much older than I was. I knew they could teach me the ropes of the game. The "old jacks" is what we used to call them. They respect me, considering that I was a young man with a lot of heart. They were like fathers and uncles to me. While all this was going on in my life at the time, I'd have a premonition that something bad would happen to me. I somehow tenuously had the feeling that I would be killed as a result of living the way that I had been. Strangely enough, I seriously began to think specifically that I'd be gunned down. This thought tormented me. It was not the fear of death. Rather, it was the element of surprise. Not knowing who would do it, or even when. I began to live in fear every day, as I constantly look over my back.

Could it be that this God whom I had come to resent was trying to tell me something?

I recall thinking that perhaps my number was up. I remember an "old jack" who didn't like me and knew the kind of lifestyle I was living said to me that my days were numbered. What he said to me stuck with me. And I believed him. It troubled me so much. Ironically, one day my Mom told me that she'd had a dream that I'd gotten killed. Despite this, my heart was still adamantly calloused. I had very little self esteem, and didn't care much as to whether I lived or died. Anticipation of death is worse than death itself. That was my mentality. I dreaded the premonition of not knowing when I'd die. As far as I was concerned, death would have put me out of my misery.

As time went on, the crew and I were still up to business as usual. We covered our territory, not allowing other gangs to peddle or distribute any drugs in our zone. We extorted anyone who dared to intrude. However, none of us was prepared for what was about to transpire.

In April of 1993, Willie and Damion covertly plotted a robbery mission which they had secretly kept to themselves. Normally, if anything in the family went down, we'd all have in on it. Those were the rules. There were no outside jobs. We were to do everything together, and to break bread together. The money we obtained, we split among ourselves. But, Willie and Damion had gone against the grain. They broke the rules and brought the heat on the family! During the course of the robbery attempt they had committed, they had killed the victim! Not only had they killed a man, but they perpetrated their mission just blocks from our hangout, which brought massive police attention and investigations on the rest of us. Although we had committed many offenses and crimes against the law, we had never killed anyone during the course of any of our operations. Willie and Damion were caught and charged with first degree murder! To the utter shock and disbelief of the family crew, we discovered their mug-shot pictures in the local newspaper! They even made the evening news! We called a meeting and voted determining that the two of them were now on their own. They would bear their own weight, all the heat, and their judgment. They had broken the rules and therefore would receive no visits, packages, nor money on their books from the family crew due to the enormity of their infraction. We decided that the show must go on. Damion and Will were from that day excommunicated from the Fulton Ave Family.

Chapter 4

Captivity

Much hadn't changed. We'd lost two soldiers due to a tremendous infraction and life sentences behind prison walls. We were now down to eight in number. Months had passed since Willie and Damion had been charged with 1st degree murder. The crew decided to start hanging rather loosely for a while. The police were on to us, applying much pressure. It was imperative to keep a low profile. We also knew that the cops in the city of Mount Vernon were corrupt. A few of their own officers were charged and sentenced to federal prison time for drug deals with known criminals on the streets. There were many young men who were also set up, or falsely framed by some of these dirty officers in uniform. I've learned that in many cases justice has her way of getting her voice heard loud and clear.

Tony, along with his brother Victor, decided to spend some time out in Brooklyn. My aunt Terry, Shawn's mom, had become extremely worried about him, suggesting that he'd move out to the state of Connecticut to start a new life. She was concerned that he'd been getting into far too much trouble, plus hanging out with the wrong crowd. We called a meeting, advising him to stay loyal, and encouraged him to keep a low profile out there. That was the last we'd ever see of my cousin Shawn. Big Mike, Chris, Trevor, Tommy, and myself chose to remain on the scene. We had to keep things going. Trevor had begun dating a lesbian girl whom he'd fallen "head over heels" for. The strength of our empire was gradually collapsing. We were falling apart at every passing moment.

It was now June of 1993. The news had gotten out that Chris had been taken into custody by authorities for questioning but later released. He indicated that the police had pictures of the entire

Fulton Ave Family, and wanted all of us badly. He'd stated that they claimed they would take us all down one by one. Just three days after Chris had this encounter, Big Mike, Tommy, and I were walking on Kingston Blvd to go to buy some cold beers. It was very hot that day. About 90 degrees. If you walked about a block or so you'd be drenched in your own sweat. Suddenly, Big Mike noticed a courier who he had employed some time ago to distribute marijuana packages for him but instead had run off with the packages and the money, skipping town. Strangely, the guy didn't notice us. We quickly plotted to confront him. Tommy then took off running up to the guy, pounding him and punching his lights out! Then, the rest of us quickly ran over to the guy and joined beating him. Witnesses began to scream and holler, "Hey, I'm calling the police, let him go, you guys are gonna kill him." Certainly, we were not going to kill the poor guy, we wanted to teach him a lesson to not fool around with anyone's money on the streets! Then, we fled the scene, leaving him laying on the ground in a pool of blood, beaten and badly bruised. We made our way to a building in the same vicinity where we decided to hide on the roof until things cooled off. While there, Tommy, the same guy who "set it off", became immensely petrified. He was scared to death. He kept on saying, "We didn't have to beat him so badly". To Big Mike and I, Tommy was getting soft! This was a sure sign of weakness. I started to think that Tommy might become a rat! Out of all the crimes we had committed together as one solid unit, no one had ever responded in the manner in which Tommy had. Big Mike and I were outraged! In fact, Tommy was a rather violent guy. I was surprised at him. I knew he was getting soft on us. I started thinking that someday Tommy would become a snitch and betray one of us. But, I didn't want to believe that notion. Tommy and I were closer than anyone in the crew. He was my right hand man. I vouched for him. I brought him in!

Later that evening I was arrested at my home and charged with assault in the 1st degree! The police indicated that I was described by witnesses as one of the perpetrators. I couldn't fathom how the authorities were able to locate my mom's residence. Somehow, they obtained leads and were able to apprehend Tommy as well. We were furious! Tommy and I were taken to the county jail in Valhalla, N. Y. Since we were co-defendants, we decided we'd take the case to trial. When the police came to arrest me, my mother's last words to me were, "You made your bed, now go lay in it." I knew then that I'd never have my mother's sympathy nor compassion at any point in my life. I knew we'd never have a meaningful relationship, which I had so longed for. I was convinced that I wouldn't have much of my Mom's support while incarcerated. But little did I know, God had major plans for me.

The fourth of July had passed. My world had stopped. Life went on for the people in the outside world, while my world was on pause. Being incarcerated was a dehumanizing experience. It takes a strong person to endure the hardships. Christ was my rock and strength. If it hadn't been for him I know I wouldn't have made it through. I had decided to let the drama between Tommy and I to cease. I felt it was best to stick together since we were in the "joint" and were co-defendants. We decided we'd have one another's back. Damion and Willie were in the same facility awaiting their transfer to the upstate "Big House" to serve their life sentence. Tommy and I had decided to stay away from them. They had broken the rules of the unit while on the outside.

Meanwhile, Tommy and I engaged in fights with other inmates, committing extortion, while rebelling against staff and correction officers. Even the "preacher man" was our target. Particularly mine. He'd come in to the jail faithfully each Sunday to share what he'd call the word of God. The minister was a tall Caucasian man. I hated him because I was so angry at God. I was also a racist. Up to that point I'd felt that the white man was the devil. My thinking was so distorted! I recall after one Sunday evening service waiting for the preacher so I could confront him. I got in his face and told him flat out that I didn't like him nor his white Jesus! I recall saying that I'd even burn the Bible! I told him that I didn't believe in his God. I went on to tell him that I was God! That minister must have thought

I was insane! I tried so hard to provoke him. I expected him to become infuriated or outraged or something. Instead, the man stood there and took it. I was baffled. My words had absolutely no effect on him. Such a glow emanated from his countenance. Sometime later, after I had gotten Saved he and I had become great friends. He'd told me that in all his years of preaching the gospel in any prison he had never encountered the opposition he experienced from me from any other inmate. I must have been demon possessed! Satan really had a strong hold on me during that dark period of my life.

As time went on, I was informed that my brother Kevin had been shot in North Carolina. He was almost killed and was in critical condition. He'd been shot multiple times with an A-K47 assault rifle! Amazingly, he survived without absolutely no disabilities. I know God spared his life for a reason. He acknowledges this truth as well, though he isn't yet saved. He would also have to serve 9 years in prison for murder subsequently after his recovery. Today he is a free man, has a son, and is doing great for himself. Furthermore, after hearing of the tragedy concerning my brother, my mother contacted me through the prison chaplain to make me aware of my father's death. My dad had lost his battle with cancer on July 13, 1994. Although we never had much of a relationship, I really felt bad for him. He was only 38 years of age when he departed this life. I didn't shed any tears. We weren't close so it really didn't affect me. The way my mom had been living her life at the time, I wouldn't have been surprised if she had joined him. I was used to not having my parents there for me. I had become conditioned to taking care of myself, looking after me and only me for reasons of survival.

Chapter 5

The Revelation of Jesus Christ

On October 3, 1993, while awaiting trial, I had an encounter that would not only affect me philosophically, but that would also change my life forever! It was a Sunday evening that I shall never forget. I was sitting in the lounge area of the day room watching a television program, which was "In Living Color", a hit comedy show during the 90's. Church services were held weekly in the library which was situated right in the middle of the day room lounge area. It was set up that way so the staff and officers could monitor everything that went on within that immediate area. By this time, church service had concluded. The other inmates who had attended service were now taking their shower. When church service was over, the minister would always stay behind to put any books or bibles that were in disarray back in place. The library, which is where service was held, had huge glass windows allowing total visibility. As I sat in my chair watching television, I turned my head away from the TV unit to glance at the minister who seemed to be taking forever to leave, (I hated every time he came, especially when he'd show those Jesus films.) I heard a voice speak to me saying in an audible fashion, "Go ask him for a Bible, now or never, you may never have another chance". It was audible but I heard it internally within my spirit. I looked around me and I saw no one. I was sitting there in that chair alone. All the other inmates were taking their shower. The staff were in the perimeter booth, from where they monitor everything via the cameras, screens, and the electronic technology available to them there.

I know the television hadn't spoken to me. I wasn't hearing things, and I know I hadn't lost my mind! That voice I heard was the voice of the Lord Jesus Christ, the risen savior who was crucified and died but arose from the dead on the third day and is alive forevermore! It was he that spoke to me! Those words he spoke came with a peace, not with any condemnation. Somehow, deep down inside my heart I knew it was God. So, I instantly obeyed. For you readers out there, I'm telling you that Jesus Christ is not dead, He is alive! If you'll just stop doubting, believe in him, call on his name, he will reveal himself to you. Now, as for me, I did not call on His name, but yet he still chose to reveal himself to me by His mercy and grace. How much more will He reveal himself to someone that calls upon His name! When the Lord spoke to me, those words permeated my spirit (proverbs 20: 27 *King James Version)*. I then immediately arose from my chair and in a blink of an eye I had my hand on the doorknob! I entered the library and there stood the preacher, on his way out to exit the library. Now, keep in mind this is the same minister that I had been opposing and persecuting. I recalled that he had been handing out those small pocket sized Gideon Bibles to inmates. So, I requested one for myself. Suddenly, there was a pause. We made eye contact. He looked at me in utter disbelief. He was absolutely stunned that I, of all inmates was asking him for a Bible. His eyes nearly popped out of their socket! He then said that he'd send it in by one of the staff if he had any left. He'd have to check his car. I waited impatiently with anticipation. Something supernatural was happening to me at that time. It was a holy moment! When that officer returned with an orange small pocket sized Gideon Bible I became thrilled! I rushed to the shower. I was never so eager to get back to my cell. I got on my knees to pray, asking God to forgive me for the life that I had lived. I asked him to help me to change, to come into my life. I also prayed that the victim of my crime would be healed and fully recover from what we had done to him. For the first time in my life I sincerely felt remorseful. After praying, I honestly felt as if a ton of dead weight had been taken off of my shoulders. I went to sleep and enjoyed the best sleep of my life, even though I was incarcerated. Such peace flooded my heart and mind. I awoke the following day with a joy that I cannot describe. You would have to be saved to know what I'm talking about! It's joy unspeakable, and full of glory (I Peter 1:8). This joy, glory, and peace is available to you if you'll open your heart to Jesus Christ right now. I became a new person in Christ (II Corin 5:17). I had such a strong desire to read the Bible. The Bible was all I could think about. Each day I would spend hours reading it. I was bubbling with joy, shinning like the countenance of angels! The glory of God was all over me. All I wanted to do was remain in my cell each day and fellowship with the Holy Spirit in the word of God and in prayer. The desire to do what I used to and to live the way I formerly had was gone. I hadn't become perfect, but I was certainly a changed individual. Please, don't be mistaken. This was not a case of "jail house religion". I had a real experience with God. I have a relationship with the Lord. And so can you. In the process of time I started leading others to faith in Jesus Christ, as well as holding Bible study services! God was using my life for His Glory! The inmates and the authorities of the facility were astonished. They could not believe what had taken place in my life.

Many thought I had lost my mind. The change that God had performed in my life was so radical that I was sent to a psychiatrist for evaluation. During the interview I shared with him my faith in Jesus and he thought I was crazy too. I tried to witness to him as well in an attempt to win him to the Lord but he opposed adamantly and quickly concluded our interview! I went back to my cell rejoicing, continuing to seek the Lord and to commune with Him in His presence. Persecution came with much intensity but with the help of God I remained steadfast in the faith, despite the rejection, ridicule, and trials. The Lord also began to do wonderful things on my behalf regarding my legal proceedings. I knew I would have to serve some time, but if God was for me, who could be against me?

Chapter 6

Judas the Betrayer

Many months had passed. The trial had begun. Tommy was up to something, but I couldn't quite put my finger on it. Was he out to save himself? Would Tommy snitch on me? You could never know the heart of another human being. Only God can discern that. I was offered a plea bargain deal of 4-12 years in state prison. This offer was made because the district attorney feared that if I had gone to trial there was a chance that I could walk. But, I decided to stay the course of the trial as my lawyer had advised. I wanted to get out of that horrible place. Although Tommy and I were co-defendants, he claimed that his attorney was working on a "special deal" to get him out, and him alone. I didn't want to believe that Tommy would sell me out, but the handwriting was clearly on the wall. Everyone else could see it except me. Quite frankly, I didn't want to. I didn't want to believe that this guy was capable of doing such a thing. However, little did I know, Tommy was about to become the district attorney's star witness to testify against me during trial. Amazingly, the victim didn't even testify against me. When he took the stand he specified that he couldn't recall if I was even involved or not. He went on to say that I was not one of the perpetrators. All he could recall was that a bunch of guys had jumped on him and beat him up for a debt he'd owed. In fact, the victim stopped coming to court all together. This left the prosecutor with no case. Sadly, he made his case off of Tommy who had become a fat sewer rat, having decided to testify against me. I did absolutely everything for Tommy while on the streets. I'd give the guy the shirt off my back. That was how close we were. I loved the guy like a brother. I know what we did to the victim was wrong. But even the victim understood he owed a debt. That's how life is on the tough streets of New York. That's probably why the victim stopped showing up in court. He knew he owed Big Mike some money. As far as the trial was concerned, he stopped showing up because he wanted to get on with his life. He didn't want to be bothered with the legal proceedings. Tommy and I both could have walked if he'd kept his fat mouth shut! But, God had a plan in all of this. If I had gotten out I would have gone back to what I was doing on the streets before I went in. God allowed me to be betrayed because in the end it would bring glory to his name! I can accept that. Just like Judas Iscariot, one of Jesus' 12 apostles who betrayed him for 30 pieces of silver. Tommy betrayed me by making a deal with the district attorney in exchange for his testimony. After testifying against me during the trial, he walked out of that courtroom smiling as a free man! I wanted to avenge myself, but God kept dealing with me about forgiving Tommy. I couldn't send the word on the streets to indicate that Tommy was a rat so that I could have someone avenge me and get Tommy back for what he had done to me because by that time the word was already out that I had become a Christian. When I got saved everyone turned their backs on me.

I was excommunicated from the Fulton Ave Family because I had become a Christian. To them I had gotten soft. I was now their enemy! I began to receive death threats by mail! The crew now wanted to take me out! They wrote letters to me saying they'd kill me if I ever got out. At the close of the trial the judge called me a piece of trash and sentenced me to 2 1/3 to 7 years. I could do a minimum of 2 years or a maximum of 7 years. I ended up serving 4 years and 5 months for assault 1st degree. My appeal was denied once, and I was denied twice for parole. I obeyed God by forgiving Tommy and decided to use the time to better myself for my advantage.

Chapter 7

The Glorious Exodus

I know now that God had a purpose for allowing me to stay in prison for the duration of the time that I did. I was supposed to be out in 2 years. I was even considered a role model inmate by the warden of the prison. I had outside clearance which enabled me to leave the jail each morning with an officer and work crew to go in to town to maintain a reservoir in the state park, clean the highways, streets, and mow lawns. I ended up staying longer due to the fact that God was preparing me to never return to such a place. He wanted to get all the "junk" out of my system. While there I made good use of my time by getting my high school diploma (GED), studying law, reading many books, including the dictionary, reading the Bible from cover to cover many times, writing, etc. In essence, I educated myself. I also sensed the call of God upon my life to the ministry. I was given a gift and an anointing to deliver the word of God in order to propagate the gospel and win souls for His kingdom. I was also given prophecies through guest ministers who had come in to the prison to minister to the inmates. God had used some of them to confirm His will for my life. I entered the prison system on June 1993. I was released January 31, 1998. I've been a free man ever since. Truthfully, it doesn't matter what you've done, where you've been in life, nor the amount of erroneous choices you may have made. God is a forgiving God. People may not be as forgiving, but as long as you make peace with the Creator, that's what matters. God can change your life if only you will believe in Him. Humble yourself. Get on your knees and ask Jesus Christ to make Himself real to you. Ask the Lord to come in to your heart and He will. I'm a new person today. I lived a rough life on the streets as a teenager. I was in and out of Juvenile Centers for youth and I spent some time in state prison for adults. I know what it's like to not have your parents there for you when you need them. But, that's when God steps in. He is a Father to the fatherless (Psalm 27:10). God can become your parent, your friend, King, provider, Lord and Savior. He can bless you, protect you, change your life and take care of you. I'm a living testimony. Since my release I've attended college, received wonderful employment opportunities, I've become a writer, a motivational speaker, and a researcher. I also compose movie scripts and newsletters to promote public awareness of current events and challenges in our world today. I am an active member in my church. God is not done with me. My life is a work in progress for His eternal Kingdom.

It is my prayer that my testimony will inspire you to believe in the very God who made Himself real to me through His son Jesus Christ, who loves us and gave Himself for our sins (Revelation ch 1: 5,6). If you believe in God but have not yet taken the next step to invite Him into your life so that you may experience a personal relationship with your Creator, I encourage you to pray the Prayer for Salvation on the following page. May God richly bless you and make himself known to you in a very powerful way!

Prayer for Salvation

Pray and repeat the following words out loud
sincerely from your heart:

Dear God, I ask that You would come into my heart, make Yourself known to me. Forgive and wash away all my sins. Cleanse me through the blood of Jesus and give me your Holy Spirit. Help me to live a life that is pleasing to You. I accept You now as my Lord and Savior. In the name of Jesus I pray, Amen.

If you have prayed the above prayer you are now saved and forgiven! Welcome to the family of God! A new and exciting life awaits you! Now you must get yourself a Bible and read the New Testament as much as possible. These are the last days so you will need to get all the knowledge about God that you can before it's too late! Be sure to talk to God each day in prayer. Find a good church to attend so that you can find new friends and fellowship with other Christians. If you will do this, your life will never be the same. Your best days are ahead!!!

CPSIA information can be obtained
at www.ICGtesting.com
Printed in the USA
LVHW090029060419
613205LV00001B/112/P